THIS BOOK BELONGS TO:

Mona

From Your Mother —
                    Christmas 95
Thought you could use this with your
                    home classes. Hope you like it.

The ABCs of Angels

The ABCs of Angels

Written and Illustrated by
Donna S. Gates

BALLANTINE BOOKS · NEW YORK

Text printed on recycled paper

Copyright © 1992 by Donna S. Gates

All rights reserved under International and Pan-American Copyright Conventions. Published in the United States by Ballantine Books, a division of Random House, Inc., New York, and simultaneously in Canada by Random House of Canada Limited, Toronto.

ISBN: 0-345-38227-7

Cover design by Georgia Morrissey

Manufactured in the United States of America

First Edition: September 1992

10 9 8 7 6 5

THIS BOOK IS DEDICATED TO

ALL THE ANGELS
IN HOPES THAT MORE PEOPLE
WILL FIND THEIR ANGEL FRIENDS!

The ABCs
of Angels

A IS FOR ANGEL.

ANGELS LOVE AND CARE FOR
YOU AND ME
WHENEVER WE NEED
THEM. ALL YOU HAVE
TO DO IS ASK!

B IS FOR BIRTHDAY.

ANGELS WERE THERE WHEN YOU WERE BORN. THEY HELPED YOU INTO THIS WORLD AND CELEBRATED YOUR BIRTH. INVITE AN ANGEL TO YOUR BIRTHDAY PARTY, THEY'D LOVE TO SEE HOW YOU'VE GROWN!

C IS FOR CAT.

ANGELS LOOK AFTER
ANIMALS TOO.
ASK YOUR KITTY
ABOUT CAT ANGELS
AND HEAR HOW
LOUD SHE PURRS...

D IS FOR DOG.

DON'T FORGET
DOG ANGELS
(OR THEIR BONES)!

 IS FOR THE EARTH.

THE WHOLE EARTH HAS
A GREAT BIG ANGEL
TO TAKE CARE OF IT.
SHE NEEDS EVERYONE'S
HELP TO KEEP OUR
EARTH BEAUTIFUL
AND HEALTHY.

F IS FOR FRIENDS.

ANGELS LOVE IT WHEN
YOU LOVE OTHER PEOPLE.
SO DO PEOPLE.
TELL A FRIEND ONE
THING YOU REALLY LIKE
ABOUT THEM AND
MAKE AN ANGEL HAPPY!
(YOU'LL FEEL HAPPY TOO.)

G IS FOR GUARDIAN ANGEL.

YOUR GUARDIAN ANGEL STAYS
CLOSE BY YOU, DOING ITS
BEST TO KEEP YOU SAFE
AND BRING YOU JOY.
LISTEN CAREFULLY,
YOU MAY HEAR YOUR ANGEL
WHISPER IN YOUR EAR!

H IS FOR HEALING.

SOMETIMES SOMETHING
HURTS SO BAD YOU CRY.
IT HELPS US FEEL
BETTER TO CRY. CALL
ON THE ANGELS TO HELP
HEAL THE HURT.
ANGEL KISSES MAKE ANYTHING
FEEL BETTER!

I IS FOR INSPIRATION.

ANGELS CAN HELP
YOU CREATE ART.

ASK AN ANGEL TO
PAINT WITH YOU TODAY!

j IS FOR JOHNNY ANGEL.

HE LOOKS LIKE A
TOUGH GUY, BUT ON THE
INSIDE HE HAS A HEART
OF GOLD. EVERYBODY'S GOT
A GOOD PLACE INSIDE THEM
NO MATTER HOW TOUGH
THEY LOOK ON THE OUTSIDE!
DO YOU KNOW ANY
JOHNNY ANGELS?

 IS FOR KOOKY.

DO SOMETHING SILLY TODAY!
PUT ON A SILLY FACE.
MAKE SOMEONE LAUGH.
YOU'LL HEAR THE
ANGELS LAUGHING WITH
BOTH OF YOU!

L IS FOR LOVE

ANGELS DON'T
EAT FOOD LIKE
WE DO, THEY LIVE
ON GOD'S LOVE.
ANYTIME YOU REALLY
FEEL LOVE, GOD'S LOVE
MOVES THROUGH YOU
AND FEEDS AN ANGEL!

M IS FOR MUSIC.

ANGELS PAINT WITH
SOUND AND SING
WITH COLORS.
LET THE ANGELS
HELP YOU MAKE
A RAINBOW
OF
MUSIC.

N IS FOR NIGHT TIME.

IF YOU
ASK THEM,
ANGELS WILL STAY
WITH YOU WHILE
YOU SLEEP.
MAYBE YOU WILL
EVEN GO ON
AN ADVENTURE
WITH AN ANGEL
IN YOUR
DREAMS...

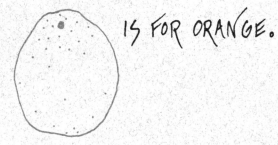 IS FOR ORANGE.

ANGELS HELP GROW
THE FOOD WE EAT.
AN ORANGE GROWN WITH
ITS ANGEL'S HELP
TASTES EXTRA SWEET.

P IS FOR PLANTS.

EVERY FLOWER,
EVERY BUSH,
EVERY VEGETABLE,
EVERY SPROUT, AND YES,
EVEN EVERY SEED
HAS AN ANGEL!

IS FOR QUIET.

YOU CAN HEAR
THE ANGELS
BEST WHEN YOU
ARE STILL.

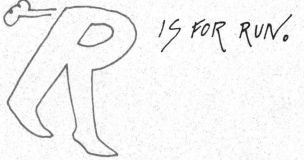 IS FOR RUN.

LET YOUR BODY MOVE!
HAVE AN ANGEL RACE
AND WATCH
EVERYONE FINISH
IN FIRST PLACE.

S IS FOR STAR.

GO AHEAD AND SHINE!
PUT ON A SHOW.
INVITE YOUR FRIENDS,
FAMILY AND THE ANGELS
TO WATCH.
ANGELS CLAP REALLY
LOUD!

 IS FOR TREE.

TREES CAN LIVE FOR A VERY
LONG TIME. JUST LIKE PEOPLE,
AS THEY GET OLDER THEY
BECOME WISER. GO TO
YOUR FAVORITE TREE, GIVE IT
A BIG HUG AND LISTEN
TO ITS WISDOM.

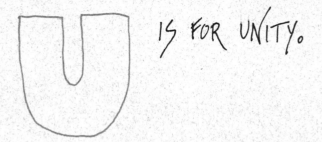 IS FOR UNITY.

UNITY MEANS
LIVING IN LOVE
WITH EVERYTHING.
UNITY MEANS
PEACE.

V IS FOR VOICE.

SING OUT
AND FEEL
JOY SWEEP IN!

W IS FOR WEATHER.

THERE ARE ANGELS
IN CHARGE OF THE WEATHER!
THEY TALK TO EACH
OTHER AND TO THE EARTH
TO FIND OUT IF IT SHOULD
BE WINDY OR STILL,
SNOW OR RAIN, CLOUDY
OR SUNNY. EACH
ONE IS VERY GOOD AT
THEIR JOB AND LIKES
TO HEAR "THANK YOU"
FROM TIME TO TIME.

X IS FOR XTRA-SPECIAL.

YOU ARE XTRA,
XTRA, XTRA
SPECIAL.

THAT'S WHY ALL THESE
ANGELS CARE ABOUT YOU!

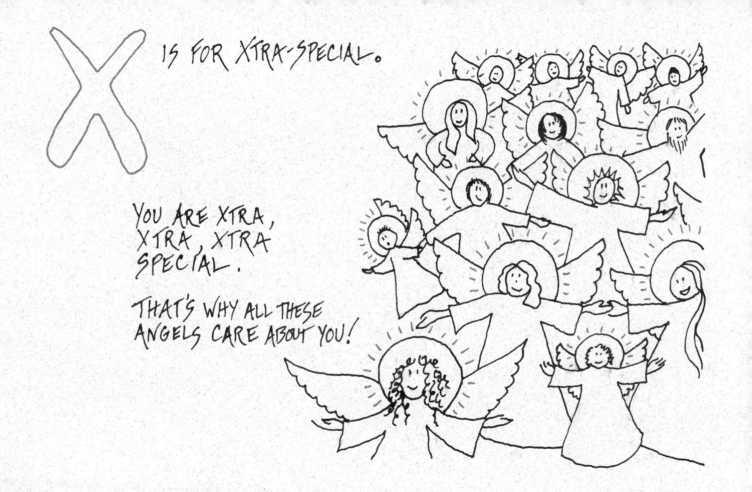

Y IS FOR YOU.

ARE YOU
AN ANGEL TODAY?

(PASTE YOUR PICTURE
IN THE HALO!)